BOLD KIDS

Panda

CHILDREN'S ANIMAL FACT BOOK

No part of this book may be reproduced or used in any way or form or by any means whether electronic or mechanical, this means that you cannot record or photocopy any material ideas or tips that are provided in this book.
Copyright 2022

All images in this book have been reproduced with the knowledge and prior consent of the artists concerned, and no responsibility is accepted by producer, publisher, or printer for any infringement of copyright or otherwise, arising from the contents of this publication.

Did you know that pandas grow to be over 5 feet long? They are about 1.5 meters long and weigh more than 300 pounds! That's nearly as large as a human. But wait, a panda isn't just a cute little pet.

A panda can live up to 20 years in the wild! And if you think a baby panda is adorable, just wait until you see one in the wild!

Did you know that adult pandas spend fourteen hours each day feeding? They consume anywhere from twelve to 38 kilograms of bamboo per day, and can sleep up to 17 hours a day! They also poop around twenty-eight kilograms per day!

It's easy to see why this beautiful, intelligent creature is loved by many people. And because they are so cute, children love to learn about them! The following facts about pandas will help them learn about this adorable animal.

Pandas live in bamboo forests between 5,000 and 10,000 feet in elevation. These bears live in a bamboo forest and make their homes out of tree stumps and logs. Their diet is low in vitamins and nutrition, so they are slow in metabolism.

Fortunately, you can see one at the San Diego Zoo! You might even be able to spot one in a circus! Don't forget to tell your kids that pandas have special thumbs that help them climb.

The panda is one of the most intelligent animals on earth! These playful bears are very smart and can solve problems with their wits. They can play ball games, use the toilet when necessary, and even use a toilet!

However, their diet is low in vitamins and nutrients, and their metabolic rate is slow. But despite their adorable looks, they have a long life span and are a great family pet.

A panda's diet is based on bamboo. It eats only bamboo. In fact, the panda has more than 20 species of bamboo. Its diet varies depending on the season and location, but it has an enormous digestive system.

Its special thumbs are the reason why pandas are so large. And it is all because of their diet that the panda has such an amazing personality.

The panda is a very endangered animal. The name "panda" may have originated from a word in Nepal that means "plant-eater". The name panda refers to the species' black and white fur. The species' white fur is an illusion that fools children into thinking that it's an ordinary cat.

But it isn't. Its eyes are so large, it's hard to see that the panda's eyes are just a distorted version of the cat's eye.

The panda is the world's cutest bear! It has pirate-style pirate-like eye patches and is black and white. It only eats bamboo and lives in bamboo forests. Its ears and legs are long enough to support the panda's long, stubby body.

A panda's ear patches are called "pandas". Its ears and tail are also long, but these animals are not as tall as a cat.

Aside from being one of the cutest animals in the world, the panda has a lot of characteristics that make it unique. For example, it is the only bear that can wear pirate-like eye patches. Its skin is black and white and only eats bamboo.

And it is the only bear that can do handstands and perform other tricks. Unlike other animals, pandas can even play ball games.

A panda's molars are flat and broad, helping it crush bamboo. Its front paws are used for chewing and cradling its cub. The panda will only leave its den for a few days. The average panda's mother weighs about 200 pounds.

It can climb more than 13,000 feet. Its baby panda can only crawl when it is three months old.

In addition to bamboo, pandas also eat fish and other small animals. This means that they eat bamboo for 99 percent of their food. That's a lot of food. But remember, pandas are omnivores. They eat bamboo, rodents, fish, flowers, and eggs.

They also eat ground meat. If you're looking for facts about a panda for kids, read on to learn more about the animal that will captivate your child's imagination.

Milton Keynes UK
Ingram Content Group UK Ltd.
UKHW050810300723
425974UK00009B/80